GEO

THE WORLD OF NASCAR

EARNING A RIDE:
How to Become a NASCAR Driver

T R A D I T I O N   B O O K S®
A New Tradition in Children's Publishing™
M A P L E   P L A I N ,   M I N N E S O T A

BY BOB WOODS

Published by **Tradition Books**® and distributed to the
school and library market by **The Child's World**®
P.O. Box 326
Chanhassen, MN 55317-0326
800/599-READ
http://www.childsworld.com

Photo Credits
Cover: Sports Gallery/Al Messerschmidt (2).
Action Sports Photography: 11
AP/Wide World: 9, 10, 13, 17
Sports Gallery: 5 (Joe Robbins), 6, 7 14, 16, 20, 22, 23 25, 26 (Al Messerschmidt)

An Editorial Directions book
Editorial Directions, Inc.: E. Russell Primm, Editorial Director; Katie Marsico and Elizabeth K.
Martin, Assistant Editors; Olivia Nellums, Editorial Assistant; Susan Hindman, Copy Editor;
Susan Ashley, Proofreader; Kevin Cunningham, Fact Checker; Tim Griffin/IndexServ, Indexer;
James Buckley Jr., Photo Researcher and Selector

The Design Lab: Kathy Petelinsek, Art Director and Designer; Kari Thornborough, Page
Production

Library of Congress Cataloging-in-Publication Data
Woods, Bob.
  Earning a ride : how to become a NASCAR driver / by Bob Woods.
     p. cm. — (World of NASCAR)
Summary: Describes the education, experience, and qualifications needed to become a driver
on the NASCAR circuit.
  ISBN 1-59187-028-3 (library bound : alk. paper)
  1. Automobile racing—Vocational guidance—Juvenile literature. 2. Automobile racing
drivers—Juvenile literature. 3. NASCAR (Association)—Juvenile literature. [1. Automobile
racing—Vocational guidance. 2. Automobile racing drivers. 3. Vocational guidance. 4.
NASCAR (Association)] I. Title: How to become a NASCAR driver. II. Title. III. Series.
GV1029.9.S74 W665 2003
796.72—dc22   2003007691

Printed in the United States of America.

**Note: Beginning with the 2004 season, the NASCAR
Winston Cup Series will be called the NASCAR Nextel
Cup Series.**

EARNING A RIDE

Table of Contents

INTRODUCTION

So, You Want to Be a NASCAR Driver?

There's a lot more to becoming a NASCAR driver than puttin' the pedal to the metal. Sure, racing team owners are looking for men—and women—who can drive real fast. But drivers also need a good understanding of how the entire car—not just the gas pedal—works. They need to communicate well with the **crew chief** and the rest of the team. They need to be physically fit. It's quite a workout handling a 3,000-pound (1,362-kilogram) road rocket blasting 200 miles (322 kilometers) per hour around a banked track for four hours. They need to be mentally tough, too, to handle the stress of racing in a tight pack of 42 other speed demons.

That's just life *on* the track. Off it, drivers have to deal with the media and the fans. They have to keep their sponsors happy. They have to find quality time for their families and friends. And if they're lucky, they'll sneak in a little peace and quiet time for themselves.

Being a fun-loving NASCAR driver may look pretty easy—especially when they're winning races. Yet, as with so many good things in life, it takes tons of hard work, determination, and dedication to reach the finish line first. Just ask Ryan

Dale Earnhardt Jr. knows what it is like to deal with the media and the pressures of being a NASCAR star.

Newman. He raced go-karts when he was a kid. Then he spent many years racing other types of cars before he was ready for stock cars. Oh, yeah, and along the way, he earned a college degree. It all paid off in 2002, however, when Ryan became the NASCAR Winston Cup Rookie of the Year.

NASCAR welcomes a fresh crop of **rookie** drivers every year. Like Ryan, they each began somewhere else. Some make it to NASCAR's major leagues. Many others don't. Let's look at what it takes to become one of those winners.

Ryan Newman's No. 12 car became a familiar sight among race leaders during his rookie season of 2002.

C H A P T E R   O N E

From Go-Karts to Stock Cars

Most kids are thrilled if they can ride a bicycle by the time they're five years old. Apparently, a two-wheeler wasn't quite thrilling enough for young Ryan Newman. "I was racing go-karts before I was five," Ryan says. He hasn't slowed down since then.

In 2002, Ryan was 24 and racing stock cars. That year, he became NASCAR's Winston Cup Rookie of the Year. The Winston Cup Series is the major leagues of NASCAR. Ryan earned his award by finish-

NASCAR Rookie of the Year Ryan Newman traveled a long road to reach his dream on the Winston Cup circuit.

ing in the top five in 14 Cup races. He also notched his first Winston Cup win when he took the **checkered flag** at the New Hampshire 300.

It was a long road that finally led to Ryan's dream season in 2002. It goes back to go-karts. In fact, many of today's NASCAR drivers started out the same way. Kevin Harvick, the 2001 Rookie of the Year, got a go-kart as a kindergarten "graduation" present. Over the next 10 years, he became a big-time winner on the go-kart circuit. Jamie McMurray raced go-karts nationally and internationally from ages 8 to 17. He won four U.S. Go-Kart titles and one World Go-Kart Championship. Casey Atwood, Ricky Rudd, and 2002 Winston Cup Champion Tony Stewart got their first taste of racing behind a go-kart wheel, too.

It's easy to see why so many future NASCAR drivers raced go-karts first. They are simple and inexpensive. A go-kart is basically a lawnmower engine bolted to a sturdy metal **chassis** [CHASS-ee]. However, they can be serious racing machines. The engines range from 5 to 40 horsepower, depending on the level

of competition. Go-karts can weigh up to about 300 pounds (136 kg) and reach speeds up to 120 miles (193 km) per hour.

Races are held on both oval and twisty road courses. This helps young drivers learn basic turning, braking, and **accelerating** skills. The World Kart Association, formed in 1971, organizes most official go-kart races in the United States. They are held nearly every weekend all across the country. They even race at the famous Daytona International Speedway in Florida.

After go-karts, Ryan worked his way up through the open-wheel racing ranks sponsored by the United States Auto Club.

Go-karts sweep through a race course. Low to the ground and powered by small engines, they can still go very, very fast.

First came the quarter midgets. "I like to call them go-karts with roll cages," he says. "I won more than 100 races in those." He also won a pair of quarter midget national championships. Those cars are one-quarter the size of midget cars, which are the next step up the racing ladder. Midgets are scaled-down versions of the cars that race at the Indianapolis 500. Ryan drove midgets for seven years, from 1993 to 1999. He won two national championships. Then he moved up to sprint cars, which are bigger and more powerful than the midgets.

Finally, in 2000, he switched to stock cars. "It was just something I always wanted to do," Ryan admits. His open-wheel racing experience was tremendous, but he still had plenty of learning to do.

This racer poses by her midget car. Midgets are "open-wheel" cars, which means that they have no fenders or metal over the tires.

LITTLE CARS, BIG FUN

Quarter midget racing is a great sport for kids. You race on oval tracks approximately one-twentieth of a mile. The cars are sturdy and fun to drive. Safety features include full roll cages, seat harnesses, and full-face helmets. The fiberglass bodies are usually painted to the driver's preference.

The Quarter Midget Association (QMA) sponsors races divided into 14 classes and age divisions, from 5 to 16. Besides weekly races, the QMA also sponsors regional races and one state championship race per region. For really serious competitors, there are three Grand National events (two asphalt track and one dirt track race) each year.

Quarter-midget cars are often driven by younger racers. Some drivers are not even old enough to drive real cars!

CHAPTER TWO

Driving Up the Ladder

"People send us **résumés** all the time on race drivers," says Roger Penske. He owns a famous NASCAR team called Penske Racing South. Penske's top driver is Rusty Wallace, a popular veteran who was the 1989 Winston Cup champion. But Penske and other owners are always looking for talented new drivers. Not just anyone will do, though. NASCAR drivers have to be the cream of the stock car crop.

As in any sport, there are many levels in stock car racing. There are amateurs who do it just as a fun hobby. At the top are the pros who dream of making it to the Winston Cup circuit. Since before NASCAR was founded in 1948, there have been hundreds of small dirt and paved tracks built all over the country. Drivers haul their race cars to a local track on Saturday nights, pay the entry fee, and wait for the green flag to drop.

Most of these "weekend warriors" don't have organized teams or sponsors to pay for cars, engines, and crews.

Some of those drivers stick with it and become really good. They race faster, harder, and smarter than their competitors. Their cars run better. They take lots of checkered flags.

Team owner Roger Penske (center) meets the media with his drivers, rookie Ryan Newman and veteran Rusty Wallace.

You might say they were born to race. But they've also worked very hard at it for years. Those are the drivers who owners like Roger Penske try to find.

Ryan tasted success by capturing the pole position at the 2002 Old Dominion 500 in Virginia.

Roger's eyes lit up when Ryan Newman's résumé crossed his desk a few years ago. Ryan had ruled in open-wheel competition. Now he was looking for a "ride" in a car with fenders. "I always wanted to race stock cars and win the Daytona 500," Ryan states. His first wish has come true. He's still working on the second one.

"I'd heard of Ryan's success in the Midwest," Roger recalls. He knew that was the same part of the country where two of NASCAR's hottest young guns, Jeff Gordon and Tony Stewart, had been open-wheel superstars, too. Roger also liked the fact that Ryan was studying vehicle structure **engineering** at Purdue University (he graduated in 2001). So Ryan was invited to join Penske Racing South in 2000 and become part of a new driving team.

All the "seat time" Ryan piled up in open-wheel cars helped him make the switch to stock car racing. "The car control experience required in [midgets and sprints] is definitely different from stock cars," he explains. "The car control

15

is key to being a better driver." Ryan also learned by talking to Rusty Wallace. "He gave me advice about racetracks where he had a lot of experience," says Ryan.

Ryan had worked on his own cars and engines for 19 years. His engineering education gave him an even better understanding of how today's high-tech race cars work. It also helped him communicate with his crew chief, race engineer, and other crew members with engineering degrees. "We have a common language and background to work with in trying to make the race car fast," remarks Ryan. Now, that's smart teamwork.

As an engineer, Ryan communicates well with his mechanics, crew chief, and pit crew.

THE ABC'S OF STOCK CAR RACING

It's hard for any newcomer to jump right into the tough Winston Cup circuit, where the world's best cars and drivers race. So many drivers—including Ryan Newman—take the "ABC" route from the minor leagues to the majors. They begin by competing in ARCA (Automobile Racing Club of America) events. Some are held at Daytona, Talladega, Atlanta, and other tracks where NASCAR runs. The next step is NASCAR's Busch Grand National Series. Pass the test there, and you're ready for Cup racing.

In 2001, Ryan's stock car education included two ARCA races, 15 Busch races, and seven Cup races. ARCA, Busch, Cup—simple as ABC.

ARCA cars resemble Winston Cup cars, but their engines are not as powerful.

CHAPTER THREE

Getting an Off-the-Track Education

F inally making it to the big-time world of NASCAR Winston Cup racing is a dream come true. It is also a huge adjustment for new drivers. The competition is tougher than in the minor circuits. All the drivers, cars, and crews are the best of the best. The pressure to win races—and money—is greater. The schedule is longer, with events held every weekend from February to November. And in between races, drivers have to test new engines, tires, and car setups. There are practice runs and qualifying events for **pole position.**

Drivers keep busy off the track, too. It costs about $12 million a year to operate a Winston Cup team. Much of that money is spent on car chassis and bodies, engines, and parts. The team

The 2002 Winston Cup championship was worth more than $25 million to Tony Stewart and his racing team.

owner has to pay mechanics, engineers, and pit crews for their work. There are offices, garages, tools, hauling trucks, and other equipment. It's expensive for the team to travel from city to city, stay in hotels, and eat.

A big part of an owner's job is to get money from sponsors to cover the team's costs. Sponsors are companies that con-

Walking billboards: See if you can count all the sponsors' logos that decorate driver Kurt Busch's racing suit and cap.

tribute money. In return, their **logos** are placed on cars and drivers' uniforms. Sponsors include companies that manufacture the stock cars: Ford, Chevrolet, Pontiac, and Dodge. Each team also has a main sponsor. Many are familiar names, such as M&M's, The Home Depot, America Online, Cheerios, and UPS. Ryan's sponsor is Alltel, a telephone company. Then there are other minor sponsors. Take a look at the various company logos on a Winston Cup car, and you'll get the picture.

Being a NASCAR sponsor is one way those companies sell their products and services. In return, the drivers are used in advertisements and make public appearances for their sponsors. Those commitments are tough on the drivers. "All the work in going to appearances and meeting with sponsors can be time-consuming," Ryan admits.

Some people say that NASCAR drivers aren't really athletes like those who play baseball, football, basketball, soccer, and other sports. NASCAR fans and drivers will tell you that that's not true. You really do have to be physically fit to drive a race

car. You need arm strength to steer the car at high speeds for up to five hours. All the shifting and braking is almost like jogging. And on a hot afternoon, it can reach 140 degrees Fahrenheit (60 degrees Celsius) inside the car!

"Being physically fit and able to recover quickly is very important," says Robby Gordon, who drives the No. 31 Cingular Wireless car. He does cardiovascular exercises to help his heart and breathing. Ryan does stretching exercises before a race to keep himself flexible and alert. Hot young driver Jimmie Johnson spends a lot of time between seasons riding his mountain bike to stay in shape. All that is just one more part of a NASCAR driver's busy life.

A NASCAR race is not a Sunday drive in the park. Ryan Newman needs a breather after a tough qualifying run.

LEARNING TO COMMUNICATE

NASCAR has become one of the most popular sports in America. Because of that, NASCAR gets lots of media attention—TV, radio, Web sites, magazines, newspapers, and books. That means the drivers have to be available for interviews, film and video tapings, and photographs. They also have to find time to mingle with fans at the track and sign autographs. "It has been different," says Ryan Newman, "but the hype goes along with being in NASCAR. You have to learn to communicate with different types of people." He believes his college education made him a better communicator. "Education is important no matter what your career is," he says.

Learning to deal with cameras, microphones, and reporters is part of being a NASCAR driver.

CHAPTER FOUR

All That Hard Work Pays Off

J amie McMurray had been a big winner in go-kart racing. When he was 17 years old, he switched to stock cars. He dominated the short tracks near his hometown of Joplin, Missouri. His winning ways continued at the I-44 and Lakeside Speedways in the Kansas City area. Jamie's luck seemed to run out, however, when he moved up to NASCAR's minor leagues. He had never won in 65 career starts in the Busch series or in 17 starts in NASCAR's Craftsman Truck series. That's one reason why his win in the UAW-GM Quality 500 in October 2002 was so stunning. The other was that it was only his second Winston Cup race ever.

So how did Jamie get a Winston Cup ride, anyway? Aren't

owners and sponsors looking for proven winners? "For people who didn't know me, it seemed like I came out of nowhere," Jamie says. NASCAR team owners Chip Ganassi and Felix Sabates knew who he was, though. "I've been a fan of Jamie's for a long time," says Sabates. He had watched a lot of his races on TV. "I like his style of driving. He's smart."

The owners had hired Jamie to race one of their Winston Cup cars beginning in 2003. But when their veteran driver, Sterling Marlin, was injured in a crash, they picked Jamie to replace him for the rest of the 2002 season. He finished 26th in his first Cup race. Then he shocked everyone a week later at Lowe's Motor Speedway in North

Jamie McMurray earned his NASCAR ride after competing in the Busch Series and racing trucks.

Carolina. In the final laps, he outraced veteran drivers Bobby Labonte, Tony Stewart, and Jeff Gordon to the finish line. He set a new NASCAR modern-era record for a driver getting his first win the earliest in a career.

Taking that first Winston Cup checkered flag is a dream come true for drivers. They race many miles and wait many years for that special moment. "Racing is something I've wanted to do my whole life," says Kevin Harvick. He raced as a kid, all the

Kevin Harvick took over the spot left after Dale Earnhardt Sr. was killed, but the young driver overcame the pressure and succeeded.

way through high school. He left college in 1997 to become a full-time stock car driver. Kevin did well in NASCAR's minor series. After Dale Earnhardt Sr.'s tragic death at the 2001 Daytona 500, team owner Richard Childress chose Kevin to take his place. In just his third start, in the Cracker Barrel 500 in Atlanta, Kevin won.

Even with Kevin and Jamie's rapid success, rookies didn't always win so quickly. Tony Stewart, the 2002 Winston Cup champion, was a newcomer in 1999. He took his first checkered flag in his 25th start. Yet Tony was the first rookie to win in NASCAR's top division since the late Davey Allison won at Talladega in 1987, his 14th start. It took Dale Earnhardt Jr. 14 starts, too, and his famous father 16 starts.

Don't be surprised, though, to see more talented young guns in the victory circle. They're racking up valuable seat time in the minors. They're communicating well with crews. They understand their high-tech cars. They're learning about sponsors. And like the owners who hire them, they want to win.

TEAM NEWMAN REIGNS IN THE RAIN

Nineteen years after he first started racing go-karts, Ryan Newman celebrated his first Winston Cup victory. It came on September 15, 2002, at the rain-soaked New Hampshire International Speedway. On lap 200, Ryan sat in the lead. Hot on his tail were Kurt Busch and Tony Stewart. The race had already been delayed twice by rain. As Ryan held off his rivals, the heavens opened up once again. Finally, NASCAR officials called the race.

Ryan was declared the winner. He thanked his family for supporting him all those years. He also recognized that winning requires a total team effort. After the race, he said, "Everybody from Penske Racing, whether it's the guy who sweeps the floor or the guy who runs the shop, did an awesome job of giving us the tools we needed to do the things we did."

After a long road to reach the top of the racing world, Ryan Newman finally tasted victory, too. Here his crew douses him after he won in New Hampshire in 2002.

STAGES OF RACING

Here are the steps, from beginning to end, that some racers move through to make it to Winston Cup racing:

- Go-karts

- Quarter midgets

- Local short-track racing

- Midgets

- Sprints

- Automobile Racing Club of America (ARCA)

- Or, some drivers go into off-road racing.

- Craftsman Truck Division

- NASCAR Busch Grand National Series

- NASCAR Winston Cup

GLOSSARY

accelerating—increasing speed

chassis—the metal skeleton or framework of a car

checkered flag—the black-and-white-checked flag that is waved as the winning driver crosses the finish line, signaling the end of the race

crew chief—the person in charge of a race team on race day who organizes the pit crew and communicates with the driver about race strategy

engineering—the study of how things are built

logo—a small design or graphic that symbolizes a company or a team

pole position—the inside spot on the front row of a race, considered the best place to start the race

résumés—documents prepared by people looking for work that list a person's previous jobs, education, and other information

rookie—a first-year player in a sport

FOR MORE INFORMATION ABOUT BECOMING A NASCAR DRIVER

Books

Owens, Tom. *Stock Car Racing.* Brookfield, Conn.: Twenty-First Century Books, 2000.

Stewart, Mark. *Auto Racing: A History of Fast Cars and Fearless Drivers.* New York: Orchard Books, 1999.

Woods, Bob. *Dirt Track Daredevils: The History of NASCAR.* Excelsior, Minn.: Tradition Books, 2002.

Woods, Bob. *Hot Wheels: The Newest Stock Car Stars.* Excelsior, Minn.: Tradition Books, 2002.

Web Sites

NBC Sports NASCAR Site
http://www.msnbc.com
Go to the main page here and click on Sports and then Motor Sports. The official NBC site features stories about recent races, interviews with drivers, and other news about NASCAR.

The Official Web Site of NASCAR
http://www.nascar.com
For an in-depth look at each track on the NASCAR Winston Cup circuit as well as statistical and biographical information on all of the drivers. Includes information on TV announcers and complete TV schedule of races.

INDEX

ABOUT THE AUTHOR

Bob Woods is a freelance writer in Madison, Connecticut. His work has appeared in many magazines, including *Sports Illustrated, Newsweek International,* and *Chief Executive.* He has written sports biographies for young readers about Ken Griffey Jr., Barry Bonds, and Shaquille O'Neal. He also wrote a children's book about the history of NASCAR and about young NASCAR drivers.